Runaway

by Jeremy Davies

Illustrated by Bruce Hogarth

The Characters

JASON

LYNN

KERRY

LYNN lives at Horseshoe Lodge, a children's home, with Mark and the others. She's worried when Mark goes missing.

JASON shares a room with Mark at Horseshoe Lodge. He decides to go and look for Mark.

KERRY doesn't take it very seriously at first when Mark runs away.

MARK dreams of living with his dad in Brighton.

MARK

Scene One

The front room of an old, empty house.

LYNN: Are you sure Mark is here?

JASON: No, I'm not. But I think he might be.

LYNN: I hope you're right. Nobody's seen him for days.

KERRY: Why would Mark hide in this old house? He said he was going to Brighton to find his dad.

JASON: He hasn't got a dad.

LYNN: Yes, he has. He's always talking about his dad.

JASON: I know.

KERRY: I don't understand.

JASON: Neither do I.

KERRY: He's mad.

JASON: No, he isn't. *(Shouting)* Mark! Are you here?

KERRY: I don't know why we're looking for him, anyway. He's nothing but trouble.

LYNN: You didn't have to come with us.

KERRY: I thought it might be fun.

JASON: Look, Kerry. Fun's got nothing to do with it. I'm worried about Mark, OK? I just want to find him.

LYNN: Me, too.

➔ *(Mark enters the room behind them.)*

MARK: Oh yeah?

LYNN: Mark! I'm so glad you're safe.

JASON: We've been worried about you.

MARK: Of course I'm safe. There's no need to worry about me. I can look after myself.

KERRY: Living in a dirty old house? You call that looking after yourself?

MARK: It's better than Horseshoe Lodge.

JASON: Are you sure?

MARK: Yes. And I wish I'd never told you about this place, Jason. Then you wouldn't have been able to find me.

LYNN: You'll have to come back, Mark, sooner or later.

MARK: Who says so?

LYNN: The police.

MARK: The police?

KERRY: They've been out looking for you.

MARK: Why? It isn't a crime to run away.

LYNN: No, but the police had to be told you were missing.

JASON:	Nobody had any idea where you were. Then I remembered this place.
LYNN:	That's why we came looking for you here.
JASON:	Come home, Mark. I know the Lodge isn't exactly Paradise, but it's where you belong.
MARK:	No it isn't. I belong in Brighton with my dad.
KERRY:	Jason says you haven't got a dad.
MARK:	That's because he's jealous. You can't believe anything Jason says, anyway. He told me he would keep this place a secret. Now he's brought you and Lynn here.
JASON:	I'm sorry I brought the girls. But I came because I'm your friend and you're in trouble.
MARK:	You're not my friend and I'm not in trouble.
LYNN:	Mark, please listen.
MARK:	You listen. Get out of here, all of you. And don't tell the police or anyone else where I am. If you do, I'll make sure you regret it.

LYNN: Come on, Jason. Let's go. Mark doesn't want our help.

JASON: I'm not going anywhere. Not unless Mark agrees to come as well.

MARK: I'm warning you, Jason.

JASON: You don't scare me, Mark.

LYNN: What about you, Kerry? Are you staying?

KERRY: Might as well. There's nothing better to do at the Lodge, is there?

LYNN: Too right.

MARK: OK. Stay if you like, but I'm never going back to the Lodge. Never!

JASON: Got any food?

MARK: What?

JASON: You must have some food and drink here. You couldn't survive without it.

MARK: I've got some crisps.

KERRY: Let's have some then. Share them out.

JASON: Is that all you've got? Crisps?

MARK: I've got some Coke as well. And I get take-aways.

KERRY: Great! Make mine a chicken curry!

LYNN: Shut up, Kerry. This is no joke.

JASON: And how long is the money for take-aways going to last?

MARK: It doesn't need to last long. I told you. I'm going to my dad's in Brighton.

JASON: When?

MARK: Soon.

JASON: You ran away five days ago.

KERRY: Yes. Why aren't you in Brighton already with your precious dad?

MARK: None of your business.

LYNN: Why don't you go now?

MARK: I'll go when I'm ready.

JASON: You'll never go, Mark. You know that.

MARK: Yes, I will! And my dad will be pleased to see
          me. We'll do everything together like we used
          to. We'll go to the football and the pictures.
          He'll get me some new clothes and we'll go
          on holiday. Abroad!

JASON: Dream on, Mark.

MARK: Just wait and see. All of you!

Scene Two

The front room of the house. Next morning. Lynn and Kelly are asleep. Jason wakes up. He looks round the room and sees that Mark is not there.

JASON: Mark? ... Mark? ... Mark?

(There is no reply.)

JASON: Oh, no. Where's he got to now? Mark!

Mark!

(Lynn and Kerry wake up.)

KERRY: For goodness sake, Jason. Why all
the shouting?

JASON: It's Mark.

KERRY: I'd guessed that.

LYNN: What about Mark?

JASON: He's not here.

KERRY: Don't tell me he's finally gone and done it!

LYNN: You mean he's gone to Brighton to see
his dad?

KERRY: Looks like it.

JASON: Fat chance! I told you. He hasn't got a dad.

LYNN: Stop going on about Mark's dad. I'm fed up with all that. I nearly froze to death sleeping in here last night.

JASON: You'll feel better after you've had some breakfast.

LYNN: What breakfast? This place isn't exactly a hotel, is it?

→ *(Mark enters the room behind them. He is carrying brown bags of take-away food.)*

MARK: Breakfast is served!

LYNN: Mark!

MARK: Muffins and coffee anyone?

JASON: You might have told us you were going out.

MARK: I don't have to tell you anything. Anyway, you were all asleep. Now are we going to eat or not?

(Mark passes round the food. They all tuck in greedily.)

KERRY: This is great!

LYNN: I feel better already.

MARK:	What about you, Jason? Enjoying the food?
JASON:	It's all right.
KERRY:	All right? It's better than the stuff we get at the Lodge.
MARK:	Come on, Jason. Admit it. You're enjoying the food.
JASON:	I said, it's all right.
MARK:	That's your trouble, Jason. D'you know that?
JASON:	What is?
MARK:	You can never admit to enjoying yourself. You're too serious all the time. You should lighten up.
JASON:	At least I don't kid myself like you do.
MARK:	What's that supposed to mean?
JASON:	You know what it's supposed to mean.
KERRY:	You mean the way he's always dreaming about living with his dad?
MARK:	It's not a dream.

LYNN: It wasn't a dream for me, either, when I lived with my dad. It was a nightmare. To tell you the truth, I was glad when they put me into care.

MARK: Glad?

LYNN: Well, not glad, exactly.

KERRY: Relieved?

LYNN: Yes. And scared at the same time. It was weird.

KERRY: I know the feeling. I felt like that when my mum gave up on me. The old bat.

LYNN: My dad's not like your dad, Mark. From what you've told us about him he seems all right.

JASON: All right? Sounds like a cross between Superman and Father Christmas to me.

MARK: What's that supposed to mean?

JASON: It means he's too good to be true.

KERRY: I never knew my dad. He must be out there somewhere, though. Not that I'll ever find him. Not so much Superman, more like the Invisible Man.

JASON: The Invisible Man! That's Mark's dad!

MARK: Don't push it, Jason.

JASON: I saw the advert in the paper, Mark.

LYNN: What advert?

JASON: The adoption advert.

MARK: Jason. Just shut up, will you?

LYNN: But they only do those adverts if they're sure that you won't ever live with your real family!

JASON: That's right. Isn't it, Mark?

MARK: What are you asking me for? You seem to know everything.

KERRY: He's always been a bit of a know-all. Haven't you, Jason?

JASON: I know this. The night Mark ran away he came into the room we share. He was upset. He had a newspaper which he threw in the bin.

MARK: Jason, please ...

JASON: Next morning he was gone. I took the newspaper out of the bin. I saw the advert. I guessed that's why Mark had run away.

MARK: They've got no right. Putting me in an advert.

LYNN: They must have talked to you about it first, Mark.

MARK: They did. But when I saw the advert, I knew I didn't want to be adopted after all.

JASON: You got cold feet, you mean.

MARK: I changed my mind. I've got a right to. I want to live with my dad, not with strangers.

(Jason takes a torn out section of newspaper from his pocket.)

JASON: *(Reading from the newspaper)* Mark is thirteen years old. He likes football and rock music.

MARK: Jason!

JASON: He is normally a cheerful, friendly boy.

KERRY: Are you sure they've got the same Mark we all know and love?

JASON: But can be moody and difficult.

KERRY: Oh yes, they have, after all.

MARK: Jason. Give me that!

(Mark tries to grab the newspaper cutting from Jason. Jason keeps it out of his reach and passes it to Lynn and Kerry.)

JASON: Here, read it for yourselves.

LYNN: When Mark was nine his mother died.

KERRY: Mark has been in care ever since.

LYNN: His father left the family home shortly after

Mark's birth, and cannot be traced.

KERRY: Mark would like to find a family who ...

(Mark grabs the newspaper from Lynn and Kerry. He tears it up.)

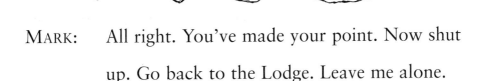

MARK: All right. You've made your point. Now shut

up. Go back to the Lodge. Leave me alone.

KERRY: Just a minute. Let me get this right. Do you

mean that after all your stories, you don't

know your father any more than I know

mine? Well, Mark?

MARK: All right. All right. So I don't know him.

That doesn't mean he doesn't exist, does it?

JASON: He might as well not exist.

MARK: But if I could just find him, meet him, see
          him, talk to him ...

KERRY: He'd ask you to live with him, would he?
          And you'd both live happily ever after? Pull
          the other one.

LYNN: Kerry! Back off will you? Can't you see
          Mark's upset?

KERRY: *(Angrily)* Anyone would think he was the only
          kid at the Lodge with a dad who doesn't give
          a monkey's.

LYNN: Kerry's right, Mark. We're all in the same
          boat, you know. You're not alone. I know it
          feels like that sometimes. But you're not.

KERRY: Get real, Lynn. Look, I've had enough of this.
          I'm going back to Horseshoe Lodge.

(Kerry goes to the door. She turns to face the others.)

KERRY: Anyone coming with me?

(The others say nothing. Kerry goes out. Then she pokes her head back around the door.)

KERRY: Oh, by the way, Mark. If you do ever go to

Brighton, don't forget to send me a postcard!

MARK: *(Slowly)* I won't be going to Brighton.

LYNN: Does that mean you've decided to come home? To Horseshoe Lodge?

MARK: I haven't got any choice, have I?

JASON: None of us have.

MARK: If I go back ... I mean, when I go back, I'll be in trouble, won't I ... for running away?

KERRY: It's a children's home, not a prison camp. You can't be shot for trying to escape.

JASON: We'll all have a bit of explaining to do when we get back. Mark, nobody can force you to be adopted. Just tell them how you feel. They'll understand.

LYNN: Well, let's go if we're going. Might as well get it over with.

MARK: Wait. Just a minute. You didn't have to come looking for me. Thanks. You're mates.

(They all make to leave.)

KERRY: You know what, Mark?

MARK: What?

KERRY: If you had gone to Brighton, I might have come with you. I like a bit of adventure.

LYNN: I think Kerry must have a soft spot for you, Mark, after all.

JASON: Come on. No more dreams. It's time to get back to reality. Isn't it, Mark?

MARK: I suppose you're right, Jason. Again!

LYNN: I don't know how you can share a room with him. He's so sure of himself.

MARK: You can get used to anything if you have to.

KERRY: Tell me about it! Now come on, let's go home.

(They leave.)